Divorc[e] Remarriage

in the 1st and 21st Century

David Instone-Brewer

Research Fellow, Tyndale House, Cambridge

GROVE BOOKS LIMITED
RIDLEY HALL RD CAMBRIDGE CB3 9HU

Contents

Biblical and rabbinic texts are translated by the author.
Rabbinic texts are prefixed with 'm' for Mishnah, 'p' for Tosephta,
'b' for Babli (Babylonian Talmud) and 'y' for Yerushalmi (Jerusalem Talmud.

The Cover Illustration is by Peter Ashton

First Impression March 2001
ISSN 1365-490X
ISBN 1 85174 459 2

1
The Divorce Texts and Their Interpretation

Jesus' Teaching

Jesus' teaching on divorce is recorded in the form of a debate with the Pharisees (Matt 19.3–9; Mark 10.2–12) and as a short saying in the Sermon on the Mount (Matt 5.31f, Luke 16.18). The version in Matt 19, which is the fullest, is translated here in a very literal way. The words which Mark does not include are in bold.

[3] The Pharisees came up to him and tested him by asking, 'Is it lawful for a person to divorce his wife **for "Any Matter?"'**

[4] He answered, 'Have you not read that he who created them from the beginning *made them male and female,* [Gen 1.27] [5] and said, *For this reason a man shall leave his father and mother and be joined to his wife, and the two shall become one flesh?* [Gen 2.24] [6] So they are no longer *two* but *one flesh.* What therefore God has joined together, let no-one separate.'

[7] They said to him, 'Why then did Moses command one to give a certificate of divorce, and to put her away?' [8] He said to them, 'For your hardness of heart Moses allowed you to divorce your wives, but from the beginning it was not so. [9] And I say to you: whoever divorces his wife, **except for "Indecency"** [Greek *porneia*], and marries another, commits adultery.'

Matthew 19.3–9

The two phrases which are in Matthew but not in Mark are also found in Matthew's version of the short saying, and not in Luke's version of the saying. This makes many interpreters think that Matthew added these phrases, while others think that Mark and Luke omitted them when they abbreviated Matthew. I will argue that Matthew added these phrases to an originally abbreviated account, and that any first-century reader would have mentally added them, just as we mentally add the word 'cigarettes' to the otherwise strange command 'Do not smoke.'

These two phrases have been translated here in a very literal way, in order to highlight the difficulties of interpreting them. The phrase 'any matter' is usually translated as 'for any cause' so that Jesus was asked, in effect, if he allowed divorce for any reason at all. The phrase 'except for indecency' is usually translated 'except in the case of adultery' or 'except on the grounds of sexual immorality,' or suchlike. There are two uncertainties with the translation of this second phrase. First, there is considerable flexibility in translating the word *porneia* because this has a very wide range of meanings, including anything from a sexual indiscretion to grievous sexual degradation. I have used 'indecency' because this word is similarly vague and wide ranging. Secondly, most translations have added words such as 'in the case of' or 'on the grounds of' which are not in the Greek text.

Although these words help to make the translation more 'flowing,' they can also obscure the meaning of the text, so I have not added them.

I have used capital letters at the start of 'Any Matter' and 'Indecency' because, as I will show below, they are actually Jewish technical legal terms. Any Jew in the first century would be familiar with these terms, just as any 21st-century person is familiar with terms like 'no-fault divorce' and 'maintenance.' For example, a first-century Jew might think that a 'no-fault divorce' was one where the legal paperwork was error-free, or that 'maintenance' referred to maintaining the singleness of a divorcee. As 21st-century readers, we are likely to suffer just as much misunderstanding, unless we can understand the legal jargon which Jesus is using, in the way that a first-century reader would have understood it.

Paul's Teaching

Paul's teaching on divorce is contained in 1 Corinthians 7 where he answered those who wanted to limit sexual relations within marriage and to divorce non-Christian partners. He said that sexual relations are an obligation within marriage (vv 3–5), and he reminded them of Jesus' teaching on divorce. He concluded that Christians should not initiate a divorce and should attempt reconciliation. However, if an unbeliever forced a divorce, the believer is 'no longer enslaved':

> [10] And to the married I command (not I, but the Lord): A wife ought not to separate herself from her husband [11] (and even if she separates herself, she ought to remain unmarried, or she ought to be reconciled to her husband); and a husband ought not dismiss his wife. [12] But concerning other matters I say, not the Lord: If any brother has an unbelieving wife, and she is content to live with him, he ought not dismiss her. [13] And a woman who has an unbelieving husband, and he is content to live with her, she ought not dismiss her husband. [14] For the unbelieving husband is sanctified in the wife, and the unbelieving wife is sanctified in the brother: otherwise your children would be unclean; but as it is they are holy. [15] But if the unbeliever separates, let them separate; the brother or sister is no longer enslaved in such [cases]: for God has called us in peace. (1 Corinthians 7.10–15)

Paul also says in v 39 that marriage is ended by death. Many interpreters have concluded from this verse (and a similar verse at Rom 7.2) that marriage can *only* end by death:

> A wife is bound for so long time as her husband lives; but if the husband should fall asleep, she is free to be married to whom she wishes; only in the Lord. (1 Corinthians 7.39)

These translations are as literal as English allows. Some translations use 'divorce' for either 'dismiss' or 'separate from,' which suggests that Paul is talking about two stages of marriage breakup—separation and divorce. However, in first-century Greek documents, both 'dismiss' and 'separate from' were used to mean 'divorce.' Paul, like any author, used a variety of words which were sometimes synonymous, and before we look for distinctions we must ask how a first-century reader would understand it.

It will be shown below that divorce in the Graeco-Roman world was enacted simply by separating from a partner or dismissing a partner, so there was no concept of a difference between separation and divorce. If Paul had meant to imply any distinction, he would have had to say so very clearly.

Traditional Interpretations

The Church Fathers followed the 'plain' meaning of these texts, that Jesus forbade all divorce, with one exception. Later Church Fathers pointed out that Paul also had one exception, though a different one. Therefore, divorce was forbidden except for 'indecency' (which was usually interpreted as 'adultery') and perhaps for desertion by an unbeliever. They also concluded that a marriage could only truly end when one partner died, which was why remarriage was equivalent to adultery. This meant that a divorcee could not remarry until a former spouse had died. The Church Fathers were virtually unanimous in this interpretation, from Hermas in the middle second century to Augustine in the fifth century, though a few, such as Tertullian and Ambrosiaster, appeared to allow remarriage for 'innocent' divorcees.

The Catholic Church and many Protestant churches followed the traditional interpretation as refined by Augustine who argued that marriage was a sacrament, because the Vulgate translated 'mystery' in Eph 5.32 as *sacramentum*. He concluded that marriage must therefore be irreversible, just as the sacraments of baptism and ordination are irreversible.

Some Reformers, such as Erasmus and Luther, allowed remarriage of a divorcee before the death of their former spouse. Luther and Calvin even allowed divorce for grounds such as refusing conjugal rights, and abandonment. *The Orthodox Church* decided to let the State deal with divorce, and recognized that divorced marriages were 'dead' so that remarriage could take place.

Modern churches follow a wide variety of practices. The Catholic Church has recently made it much easier to seek an annulment, which means that the former marriage can be declared as never having occurred, so another marriage will not really be remarriage. Other churches allow the State to decide who divorces and still others allow divorce for reasons which are not immediately obvious in Scripture. A few churches allow no divorce at all.

Modern Interpretations

Pastorally-minded theologians have tried to find ways to allow divorce for those suffering physical and emotional abuse. Some have done this by broadening the two exceptions which were stated by Jesus and Paul, while others regard the New Testament as a source of principles rather than strict regulations. Thus

David Atkinson[1] broadened Jesus' exception to include anything which ruined a marriage and Stephen Clark[2] widened Paul's exception to a similar degree. Other interpreters suggest that Jesus and Paul were simply teaching the principle that marriage should continue if possible, and that each gave different examples of permissible grounds for divorce.

A further area of discussion is the question of resolving the differences between Mark's and Matthew's versions of Jesus' teaching. Scholars generally assume that Mark's version is oldest, and that Matthew or the church later added the exception for 'indecency.' This implies that Jesus did not allow any divorce at all, which fits in with Jesus' other uncompromising and idealistic teaching such as 'turn the other cheek' and 'do not ask for repayment.'

One difficulty with removing Matthew's phrases is that it makes the Pharisees' question relatively meaningless. They ask: 'Is it lawful for a man to divorce his wife?' This should prompt the answer: 'Of course, because the Law says so!' (in Deut 24.1). The wording in both gospels clearly implies that they were asking Jesus his opinion of what the Law meant, and in particular Deut 24.1 because this was the only text which mentions a divorce certificate which they refer to in the debate.

The question might make sense, however, if a group of Jews existed which forbade all divorce and remarriage, so that the Pharisees were asking if Jesus sided with them. When the Dead Sea Scrolls were first discovered, J A Fitzmyer[3] and others thought that they had found such a group. However, the texts which they relied on (CD 4.20f; 11QTemple 57.15–19) are now generally regarded as a criticism of polygamy and not divorce or remarriage.[4]

The question would also make sense without Matthew's addition if the Pharisees knew that Jesus forbade all divorce, because the question would be one way to point out that his teaching was contrary to the Law. This would mean that Matthew's exception for adultery was not uttered or even implied by Jesus. This introduces a new problem for those who regard Scripture as inspired, because Matthew would be dramatically changing the teaching of Jesus. Therefore some scholars have tried to show that Matthew's additions were implied by Jesus' teaching, or could at least fit in with the spirit of his teaching.

Joseph Bonsirven[5] and others suggested that *porneia* ('indecency') meant 'illegitimate marriage,' so that in Matthew Jesus allowed remarriage only for those who were not validly married. However, in normal Greek usage, *porneia* meant

1   *To Have and To Hold: The Marriage Covenant and the Discipline of Divorce* (London: Collins, 1979).
2   *Putting Asunder: Divorce and Remarriage in Biblical and Pastoral Perspective* (Bridgend, Wales: Brynterion Press, 1999).
3   'The Matthean Divorce Texts and Some New Palestinian Evidence,' *Theological Studies* 37, 1976, pp 197–226.
4   David Instone-Brewer, 'Nomological Exegesis in Qumran "Divorce" Texts,' *Revue de Qumran*, 18, 1998, pp 561–579.
5   *Le Divorce dans le Nouveau Testament* (Paris: Société de S Jean l'Evangékuste, Desclée and Die, 1948) esp pp 46–60.

general sexual immorality, especially prostitution and adultery. Therefore, if Matthew had meant to give such a restrictive meaning to the term, the context would have to make this very clear.

R H Charles[6] argued that Jesus presented his teaching on divorce while the Jews still had the authority to apply the death penalty for adultery, as the Old Testament law demanded. In this situation, there was no need to allow divorce in the case of adultery, because the marriage would end when the death penalty was imposed. He pointed out that the situation changed greatly when the Jews lost the right to impose capital punishment, which occurred in 30 CE, according to rabbinic traditions.[7] He said that Matthew was aware that adulterers would go unpunished if they could not be divorced, so he added the exception in the spirit of Jesus' teaching. However, it is generally accepted that the rabbinic traditions are unlikely to be accurate in this case, and that the death penalty probably ended in 7 CE when the Roman government of Palestine began. Also, rabbinic traditions suggest that few adulterers, if any, were punished with death in the first century, except occasionally through mob violence.

A suggestion by I Abrahams[8] and others, which was popularized by William Heth and Gordon Wenham[9] and more recently by Andrew Cornes,[10] was that Jesus allowed divorce for adultery because it was, in any case, compulsory in Judaism. They maintained that Mark, who was writing for Gentiles, did not include this exception because divorce for adultery was not compulsory outside Judaism. But divorce *was* compulsory for adultery in Graeco-Roman law,[11] though in practice this was unenforceable in both Graeco-Roman and Jewish law. We now know that Judaism was extremely diverse in the first century, and unpopular Pharisaic rules were often ignored. Also it is uncertain that Mark's version was written for Gentiles. It is argued that Mark mentions a woman divorcing her husband, whereas in Judaism only men could initiate divorce. However, a recent papyrus has shown that Jewish women *were* in fact able to divorce their husbands, and so Mark could have been writing for a Jewish audience after all.[12]

These various proposals have failed to find a context in which the Pharisee's question would be meaningful without Matthew's additions. They have also failed to show how Matthew's additions could concur with a 'no-divorce' teaching. Therefore Matthew has either changed Jesus' teaching, or (as I will argue below) he has correctly added the words which were implicit for any first-century reader. We will now examine how a first-century reader would have understood this teaching.

6   *The Teaching of the New Testament on Divorce* (London: Wiliams and Norgate, 1921).
7   '40 years before the destruction of the Temple,' bSanh.41a.
8   *Studies in Pharisaism and the Gospels* (London: Macmillan, 1917).
9   *Jesus and Divorce* (London: Hodder and Stoughton, 1984).
10 *Divorce and Remarriage: Biblical Principles and Pastoral Practice* (London: Hodder & Stoughton, 1993).
11 The *lex Julia de maritandis de ordinibus*, 18 BCE and *lex Papia Poaea nuptialis*, 9 BCE.
12 David Instone-Brewer, 'Jewish Women Divorcing their Husbands in Early Judaism: The Background to Papyrus Se'elim 13,' *Harvard Theological Review* 92, 1999, pp 349–57.

2
How First-Century Jews
Would Have Understood Jesus

First-Century Interpretation

To understand the meaning of the New Testament, we often have to read it through the worldview of a first-century Jewish or Graeco-Roman convert. For instance, it is difficult to understand Jesus' criticisms of the Pharisees in Matthew 23 without studying Jewish laws about tithing and cleanliness, and it is impossible to understand Paul's abhorrence of women who uncover their heads in public unless one realizes that this was an ancient equivalent of going topless.

The Hillelite and Shammaite Debate

Since the mid-19th century, most scholars have recognized that the extra phrases in Matthew's account refer to a debate between two groups of Pharisees in the early first century. The Hillelites introduced a new 'no-fault' divorce called 'Any Matter.' This was based on their interpretation of a phrase in Deut 24.1 which the Shammaites interpreted as 'Indecency.' Rabbinic traditions recorded a summary of this debate:

> The School of Shammai says: A man should not divorce his wife *except* if he found *indecency* in her, since it says: *For he found in her an indecent matter* (Deut 24.1).
> And the School of Hillel said: Even if she spoiled his dish, since it says: *[Any] matter* (Deut 24.1).[13]

The dispute concerned the phrase 'a matter of indecency' (Hebrew *ervat davar*). The Hillelite Pharisees interpreted the phrase as two grounds for divorce: 'Any Matter' and 'Indecency,' whereas the Shammaites interpreted it as a single ground for divorce, 'Indecency.' The Hillelite position could be summarized as 'Any Matter,' because this one ground included the second ground 'Indecency.' The Shammaites emphasized that there was only one ground for divorce in this text, so they summarized their position with the phrase 'nothing except Indecency.' Matthew added these two summaries to his account, implying that the debate went as follows:

The Pharisees asked Jesus: 'Does the Law (*ie* Deut 24.1) allow divorce for "Any Matter"?' (the Hillelite interpretation). He replied, after a long digression, that this text allowed divorce for 'nothing except "Indecency"' (the Shammaite interpretation). This meant that those who were divorced for 'Any Matter' were

---

13 Sifré Deut 269, ed Finkelstein 288. *cf* mGit.9.10; ySot.1.2, 16b.

not validly divorced, so they were theoretically still married. Therefore, 'if they marry another, they are committing adultery.'

Matthew was correct to add these phrases to his account, because any first-century Jewish reader would have mentally done likewise. The older version, which is preserved in Mark and Luke, did not contain these phrases because they would be superfluous. They may not even have been spoken in the original debate, because they were obvious in this context for any first-century Jew.

To use a modern example, imagine someone asking, 'Is it lawful for someone under 18 to drink in this country?' It would be superfluous to add the words 'alcoholic beverages,' even though the question is meaningless without them. Similarly, the question 'Is it lawful for a man to divorce his wife?' was meaningless, because Deut 24.1 clearly permitted it. Therefore any first-century Jew would add the obvious words 'on the grounds of "Any Matter."' These words were obvious because they referred to a well-known and current legal debate.

By the second century, however, this was far from obvious. The destruction of Jerusalem in 70 CE resulted in the end of the Shammaites and the triumph of the Hillelites, who took over all legal and religious institutions. Before 70 CE, this debate was very well known, because any seeking a divorce had to choose a judge who would allow the type of divorce they wanted. If they wanted an 'Any Matter' divorce, they had to make sure they went to a Hillelite. After 70 CE the question had no practical importance because everyone in authority was Hillelite.

The historical context of the gospel accounts was therefore lost to the early Church Fathers and succeeding generations of Christians, though it was preserved in the legal records of early rabbinic scholars.

Other Grounds for Divorce in First-Century Judaism

Before the invention of 'Any Matter' divorces, a Jew could only get a divorce for a limited number of grounds which had to be proved in court if they were disputed, so they often entailed embarrassing public accusations. The 'Any Matter' divorces did not require any proof or court appearances so they soon became very popular. The traditional Old Testament grounds for divorce were:

1) Deut 24.1: 'an indecent matter,' that is, adultery;
2) Gen 1.22, 28: 'be fruitful and multiply.' The Jews thought that this command made infertility a ground for divorce, and they applied it also to blemishes which made the person repulsive to their partner;
3) Exod 21.10f: 'you shall not diminish her food, clothing or love.' This text referred originally to a slave wife when a man took a second wife. The lawyers argued that if a slave wife had these rights, then so did a free wife and so did a husband. These three rights became grounds for divorce if a husband or wife neglected their spouse's material or emotional support, or subjected their spouse to physical or emotional abuse.

A husband had to provide food, cloth or money, and the woman had to make them into meals and clothing. The neglect of 'food, clothing or love' were the main grounds for divorce before the 'Any Matter' divorce was introduced, and even a woman could gain a divorce on these grounds. If she convinced a court that she had been neglected, it would force her husband to write out a divorce certificate.[14]

Jesus on Marriage

When Jesus was asked his opinion about the 'Any Matter' divorces, he did not immediately answer the question. He used the occasion to speak about marriage, which he considered more important than divorce, and to point out several areas where he disagreed with his Jewish contemporaries. He may also have taught about other aspects of marriage where he agreed with normal Jewish teaching, such as the importance of mutual love and respect, but the abbreviated gospel accounts would not be expected to include this. The gospels record the following areas where Jesus disagreed with contemporary Jewish teaching:

1) *Marriage is monogamous.* The Old Testament allowed polygamy (it is assumed in Exod 21.10, Deut 21.15 and Lev 18.18) and it was still permitted in first-century Palestine. But Jesus said that monogamy was the Old Testament ideal.
2) *Marriage is designed to be lifelong,* so divorce should be avoided if at all possible.
3) *Marriage should only be ended by divorce in cases of 'hard-heartedness' (ie stubbornness).* Jesus did not explain what he meant by this, but his listeners would probably think about Jeremiah 3–4, because this is the only passage which uses 'hard-hearted' in the context of marriage or divorce.[15] Jeremiah described Israel as God's 'hard-hearted' wife when she repeatedly committed adultery with the idols, and stubbornly refused to repent. The Old Testament prophets said that God eventually had to divorce Israel (see below) but only after many attempts to get her to repent. Presumably Jesus meant that one should not immediately seek to divorce an erring partner, but one should invite repentance. However, divorce is reluctantly permitted when there is a hard-hearted refusal to repent. This agrees with Jesus' teaching that we should forgive those who repent (Luke 17.3f).
4) *Marriage should even survive adultery, when possible.* The Pharisees said that Moses 'commanded' divorce for 'Indecency,' whereas Jesus said that Moses merely 'allowed' it. This distinction is obscured in Mark, and it is possible that Matthew invented it, though it fits very well into the historical context, because the Pharisees tried to make divorce compulsory after adultery. Jesus wanted to emphasize that divorce was permissible but not compulsory when there was a valid ground. Unlike the Pharisees, he encouraged people to seek repentance from their partner and then forgive them, even in a case of adultery.
5) *Marriage is not compulsory.* This teaching in found in Matthew immediately after the debate on divorce (Matt 19.10–12). Jesus said that a man may choose to be a eunuch—live a celibate life—whereas Rabbinic Judaism taught that

14   mArak 5.6; mKe 7.10.
15   Jer 4.4 LXX.

'go forth and multiply' was one of the 613 commands of the Law which every man had to strive to fulfil.[16] Since Jesus repudiated this interpretation, he presumably also repudiated the Jewish use of infertility as a ground for divorce, which relied on this interpretation.

Jesus on Divorce

The Pharisees eventually brought Jesus back to their question. Whilst Matthew made it clear that Jesus was answering a question concerning the interpretation of Deut 24.1, the original readers of the older account in Mark and Luke did not need to be reminded about the context of the debate. However, by the time the gospels reached their final form, some editorial additions such as those in Matthew would have been useful.

Jesus made it clear that he sided with the Shammaites. This does not mean that he was a Shammaite, because he usually sided with the Hillelite position on other matters. Jesus was an independent interpreter whose opinion sometime agreed with views already stated elsewhere. He disagreed with both of these schools and with most other branches of Judaism with regard to several other matters, as we have seen.

Jesus' words 'Those whom God has joined, let no-one separate' have often been misunderstood as a statement of impossibility, as if it said: 'Those whom God has joined *cannot* separate.' In both Matthew and Mark, the verb 'separate' is in the imperative, which indicates a command or a plea, *ie* 'Please do not separate' or 'You must not separate!' Both of these imply that it is *possible* for couples to separate but they should not do so.

Therefore Jesus was not condemning 'any divorce' (as most translations imply) but divorces for 'Any Matter'—the new type of divorce which was introduced by the Hillelites. He allowed divorce for 'Indecency,' though he discouraged it. He said that the popular divorces for 'Any Matter' were invalid, so they were still married. Therefore, if they remarried they were actually committing adultery.

The Shorter Accounts

How do we make sense of the shorter accounts of Jesus' teaching in the light of the longer acounts, and especially that of Matthew?

The shortest summary of Jesus' teaching (in Luke 16.18) said simply that anyone who divorced and remarried was committing adultery. Despite the very substantial abbreviations, this was still essentially correct for all practical purposes. Strictly speaking, Jesus only condemned the 'Any Matter' divorces, but this included virtually all divorces which took place in first-century Palestine. So, in effect, Jesus said that all divorces were invalid, and anyone who remarried had committed adultery.

We should expect abbreviations in the gospel account of the debate because it

---

16 The House debates in mGit.4.5 and mYeb.6.6 shows that this was an early doctrine.

is clearly not verbatim and rabbinic debates used similar abbreviation.[17] This is seen especially clearly in the debate about divorce. The abbreviated account in *Sifré* (which was cited in the section on 'The Hillelite and Shammaite Debate' above) is further abbreviated in *Mishnah Gittin*:

> The School of Shammai says: "A man should not divorce his wife *except* if he found a *matter of 'Indecency'* in her, since it says: *For he found in her an indecent matter* [Deut 24.1]." And the School of Hillel says: "Even if she spoiled his dish, since it says: *For he finds in her an indecent matter* [Deut 24.1]."[18]

The later account in the *Jerusalem Talmud* is even shorter:

> The School of Shammai says: A man should not divorce his wife *except* if he found *'Indecency'* in her.[19]

It is noteworthy that the wording of the Shammaite viewpoint in these two versions is exactly equivalent to the two versions in Matthew:

> Every one who divorces his wife, *except* for a *matter of 'Indecency'*…(Matt 5.32)
> Whoever divorces his wife, *except* for *'Indecency'*…(Matt 19.9)

There is much more which Matthew and the rabbinic traditions could have added to their accounts of this debate, including mention of the other Old Testament grounds for divorce which everyone agreed on. They were not mentioned in this debate because they were not subject to dispute, and an account of a debate only needs to mention the differences between each side.

The gospels normally omit to mention things on which all Jews agreed. They never record Jesus forbidding polytheism or sex before marriage, as all branches of Judaism already condemned these. However, the epistles did teach against these things because they were addressed to a non-Jewish world. But where Jesus disagreed with the *status quo*, the gospels do appear to record his teaching.

The same was true for rabbinic debates, which only mentioned differences between the two sides. When one reads the debate about divorce, one might conclude that the Shammaites only allowed divorce for 'Indecency.' However, we know that they also allowed divorce for other Old Testament grounds which all branches of Judaism in the first century accepted. We will now look at those other grounds, and then consider why Jesus was silent about them.

God as a Divorcee

The principle behind the Old Testament grounds for divorce was that marriage was a contract, and the terms of the contract were the marriage vows or obligations. If either partner broke these terms, the other partner could choose to end the contract if they wished—that is, to get a divorce. This emphasized that the sinfulness of divorce lay in the breaking of marriage vows, and not in the process of divorce. Therefore Malachi defined divorce as 'treachery against your companion, the bride of your contract' (2.14).

---

17   Birger Gerhardsson, *Memory and Manuscript*, Acta Seminarii Neotestamentici Upsaliensis 22 (Uppsala, 1961).
18   mGit 9.10.
19   ySot 1.2, 16b.

The provision of 'food, clothing and love' were terms in a marriage contract and they were specifically quoted as such in several ancient Jewish marriage contracts. One example of a divorce which cited these grounds was the description of God's divorce from Israel by the Old Testament prophets. They described God divorcing Israel and later temporarily separating from Judah (Hos 2.2; Jer 3.1–5; Is 50.1).[20] Ezekiel listed the marriage vows which God had kept but which Israel had broken: God loved Israel and he provided food and clothing, but Israel used them to feed and clothe her lovers, the idols, with whom she also committed adultery (Ezek 16.16–19). Jeremiah said that Israel stubbornly refused to repent, and he called her 'hard-hearted' (Jer 4.4 LXX). Although God was the innocent party in this divorce, he still experienced the painfulness of divorce first hand and concluded 'I hate divorce' (Mal 2.16).[21]

Jesus' Silence on other Grounds for Divorce

It is clear that Jesus condemned the Hillelite 'Any Matter' divorces and accepted divorce for adultery, but what did he think about the other Old Testament grounds for divorce? It is possible to argue that he agreed with these other grounds, because otherwise he would not be silent on this matter. An argument from silence is always precarious, but it may be defensible on this occasion, because his silence is so surprising. Jesus was asked about a specific issue (the 'Any Matter' divorces) but before giving his opinion on this, he spoke about a large number of other matters concerning marriage and divorce where he disagreed with some or all branches of Judaism. In the light of this, it is very significant that he failed to mention the other grounds for divorce which were accepted by both the Hillelites and Shammaites.

When Jesus denied the validity of divorce on any grounds 'except for "Indecency"' this did not imply that 'Indecency' was the only allowable ground in Scripture. The Shammaites used exactly the same phrase, and we know that they also allowed other types of divorce.[22] The Shammaites meant that 'there is no ground for divorce in Deut 24.1 except "Indecency."' They did not mean that 'there is no ground for divorce in all Scripture, except "Indecency."' It would be extraordinary if Jesus meant something completely different, when he used the same words in the same context, to the same group of people. It is likely that Jesus, like the Shammaites and all other Jews, accepted the validity of divorces for neglect of 'food, clothing or love.'

Jesus was silent on these three obligations—but Paul was not.

---

20   God spoke the Ancient Near Eastern divorce formula to Israel (Hos 2.2). Jeremiah worried that God could never remarry her (Jer 3.1–5). God said that he had not divorced Judah and was willing to have her back (Is 50.1; 54.5–10).

21   The translation of this and the surrounding verses has many problems—see G P Hugenberger, 'Marriage as a Covenant: A Study of Biblical Law and Ethics Governing marriage, developed from the perspective of Malachi,' *V T Supp* 52 (Leiden, New York: Brill, 1994).

22   The debate in mKet 5.6 shows that they regarded the neglect of 'love' in Ex 21.10f as a ground for divorce. Presumably they also accepted the other two grounds in that text.

3

How First-Century Converts Would Have Understood Paul

First-Century Graeco-Roman Culture

The New Testament epistles were largely written to a mixture of Greeks and Jews who lived outside Palestine, under the Graeco-Roman legal system.

The most common end to marriage in the first-century Graeco-Roman world was 'divorce-by-separation.' This was enacted simply by separating—by mutual agreement, desertion, or dismissal (depending on who owned the marital home). Neither party had to give a reason for ending the marriage, and if one partner wanted the divorce, the other was powerless to stop it. There was no concept of separation without divorce or separation preceding divorce and, unlike in the modern world, there was no concept of a minimum period of separation or desertion. Separation was considered to be the proof that divorce had occurred, even if neither partner had declared their intention to divorce.

In the matter of remarriage, the Graeco-Roman and Jewish world were very similar to our own. Anyone who had a valid divorce had an automatic right to remarry. In fact the main purpose of a divorce certificate was to state this right. The only compulsory words on a Jewish *get* or divorce certificate were: 'You are now free to marry any man you wish.'[23] Very similar words occurred on most Graeco-Roman divorce certificates, though they rarely bothered to write a certificate. As soon as a couple separated, either partner was free to remarry.

Paul on Marriage

Paul, like Jesus, was more interested in marriage than divorce. When some at Corinth wanted to divorce their unbelieving partners, Paul reminded them of their obligations within marriage.

1) *Conjugal Obligations* (1 Cor 7.3–5). We normally speak of conjugal rights, but Paul spoke about obligations. He said that each partner should regard themselves as the servant of the other. This language of 'service' and 'authority' is reminiscent of Exodus 21.10f, on which this obligation is based. The Pharisees discussed how long a couple could abstain from conjugal relations on the basis of this text,[24] while Paul was concerned about the reason for separation. He said that it should only be for the sake of extra prayer time.

2) *Material Obligations* (1 Cor 7.33–34). Paul said that married people should be concerned about the 'things of this world,' so that they 'please' their husband or wife. Surprisingly, Paul spoke positively about 'the world' because mate-

23   mGit 9.3
24   mKet 5.6

14

rial support was commanded in Exod 21.10f ('food and clothing'). However, he did suggest that this obligation might distract a believer from serving God, which is why he chose to remain single. The Pharisees discussed the exact amount of food and clothing which the man had to provide, and the amount of sewing and cooking which the woman had to perform. Paul, in contrast, turned his back on this legalistic approach. Instead of speaking about how much food and clothing were required, he said that they should seek to 'please' their husband or wife.

3) *Believers should only marry believers*, if they have the choice. The Corinthian church were all first generation believers, and some came from cultures where parents chose their spouse, so very few had been able to choose a believer. Therefore Paul said that a widow or widower should marry 'only in the Lord' (1 Cor 7.39) though this presumably also applied to any other single younger people from Christian families.

Paul on Divorce

Paul was mainly concerned to stop believers from divorcing their unbelieving spouses, which some believers at Corinth were advocating. He also made some other general rulings about divorce.

1) *Believers should not use divorce-by-separation* (1 Cor 7.10–14)—the Graeco-Roman form of no-fault divorce. Paul told the Corinthians that they must not 'separate themselves' from their spouse. He appealed to the teaching of Jesus who condemned the no-fault divorce in Judaism—the Hillelite 'Any Matter.'

2) *If they have used divorce-by-separation, they should attempt to reverse it* (1 Cor 7.11). Some (or perhaps one) of the Corinthians had already divorced their unbelieving partner by separating from them. Some translations suggest that the woman 'has *been* separated' (passive), but the same Greek form can also mean 'has separated herself' (reflexive). The reflexive makes more sense because if her spouse had chosen to divorce her, there would be little point in telling her to be reconciled.

3) *If they have been victims of divorce-by-separation, they are 'no longer enslaved'* (1 Cor 7.15). Whether or not this implies remarriage (see below), their marriage is certainly over. Once someone's spouse has walked out or dismissed them, the divorce has been fully enacted. The only thing the victim can do is to make sure the dowry is returned and that nothing has been stolen from their house.

4) *There are valid grounds for divorce.* Paul condemned the no-fault divorce-by-separation, but he implied in v 15 that desertion was a valid ground for divorce. He did not state any other grounds for divorce, but presumably he also allowed divorce for adultery, in accordance with Jewish law, Graeco-Roman law and the teaching of Jesus.

Did Paul allow these other Old Testament grounds for divorce? It is not clear, but he did affirm them as obligations within marriage (1 Cor 7.3–5, 33–34).

Paul on Remarriage

Some commentators have found a reference to remarriage in 1 Cor 7.27 where Paul says that a person who is 'freed' from marriage may get married. However, the context is ambiguous, and the person may have been 'freed' from a betrothal.

The phrase 'no longer enslaved' is also ambiguous for a modern reader, though it would have only one meaning for a first-century reader. Modern interpreters have argued whether it means a freedom to remarry or merely the freedom to remain separate. However, someone who had been divorced-by-separation had no choice but to remain separate. Once their partner had left them, the divorce had already taken effect, with the full force of Greek and Roman law to enforce it. Also, to a first-century reader, the phrase would remind them of the wording in Jewish and Graeco-Roman divorce certificates—'You are now free to marry any man you wish.'

The phrase 'no longer enslaved' is especially apt to a divorce certificate which was frequently compared to a certificate of emancipation from slavery.[25] The two documents had similar wording and similar administrative procedures. Also, in some ways, a woman divorcee *was* like an emancipated slave—for the first time she could choose how to spend her money, do business on her own behalf, and generally live life as she wished. She could even choose a husband by herself.

The only compulsory words on a divorce certificate were: 'You are now free to marry any man you wish.' Paul quotes these words in 1 Cor 7.39, when he wants to establish the right of a widow to remarry. Remarriage was a fundamental right of a divorcee, because she had a certificate proving this right, whereas a widow often had to provide her own proof that her husband was dead.[26]

When Paul said 'you are no longer enslaved' to someone who had been deserted, first-century readers would therefore assume that he was speaking about their freedom to remarry. In fact this was so obvious that they might even consider it pedantic to state this freedom.

No Remarriage Till Death Occurs?

Paul says in two verses that a marriage ends when one of the partners dies (1 Cor 7.39; Rom 7.2). However, neither of these verses state that marriage *cannot* end with divorce, and neither of them indicates that death is the *only* way to end a marriage. They do not mention divorce because it does not fit into the context. The context of 1 Cor 7.39 concerns the rights of a widow, so divorce is naturally not in view.

Romans 7.1–4 is a metaphor about Jesus and the Law. Paul says that the Jewish convert is like someone who wants to marry Christ but who is still married to the Law. The believer has no grounds for divorce because the Law never breaks any marriage vows. Their only hope is that the marriage will end in death. But

---

25 Early references are in mGit 1.4; 9.3.
26 A conscientious husband often gave a wife a conditional divorce certificate before going on a long journey, so that if he did not return she could use the divorce certificate rather than try to find proof that he was dead. See mGit.7.7–9.

the Law will not die. The good news is that the converts share the death of Christ, which ends their marriage to the Law, and frees them to marry Christ.

None of this implies that marriage can only end by death, because neither context suggests that Paul is providing an exhaustive list of the ways in which a marriage can end.

Husband of One Wife?

The Pastorals say that a church leader should be 'a man of one woman' (1 Tim 3.2) and the corresponding phrase 'a woman of one man' occurs in relation to widows (1 Tim 5.9). These are usually translated 'a husband of one wife' and 'wife of one husband.' The first phrase has been interpreted in many different ways, with the corresponding interpretation for the second:

a) a church leader must be married, or
b) he must not be a polygamist, or
c) he must not remarry till his ex-wife has died, or
d) he must not be a womanizer.

The first interpretation is contradicted by Paul and Jesus who both speak highly about the unmarried state (1 Cor 7.7f, Matt 19.12). The second is impossible because, even where polygamy was allowed, only men were permitted more than one spouse, so the parallel phrase 'woman of one man' would not make sense. The third is also unlikely; it could not mean that they were forbidden to remarry, because the Pastorals encourage widows to do so (1 Tim 5.14, *cf* 1 Cor 7.27, 39), so some have suggested it might mean remarrying while a former spouse lives. If the indissoluble view of marriage is correct, a remarried person is still married to a former living spouse, so they would have two husbands or wives.

An early Graeco-Roman reader, however, would naturally think of the last meaning. It was similar to the Latin *univira*, 'a one-man woman.' The term is found in inscriptions and funeral orations concerning women who were faithful to one man throughout their lives. This relatively rare faithfulness was highly prized and honoured. The corresponding 'one-woman man' is not found in the first-century Graeco-Roman world, because it would not carry similar honour. It was considered normal for a man to have a mistress, and many also had a live-in concubine.

Therefore the Pastorals are not saying that a church leader had to be married, or that they must not be remarried, but that they had to be sexually moral. They had to be 'a man of one woman' or 'a woman of one man'—that is, faithful to their marriage partner.

4
Summary of the First-Century Interpretation

First-century Jewish hearers and readers of Jesus' words came to the subject of divorce and remarriage with several presuppositions. All branches of Judaism were agreed that there were five grounds for divorce in Scripture: infertility (Gen 1.22, 28), unfaithfulness (Deut 24.1), and neglect of food, clothing or love (Exod 21.10f), and that these were recognized as the vows implicit in a marriage contract. The Old Testament example of God's divorce from Israel illustrated that divorce occurred when these vows were repeatedly and stubbornly broken. They also learned from Scripture that remarriage was allowed after divorce (Deut 24.1–4), and the purpose of the divorce certificate was to state this right. The Hillelites had popularized a new no-fault divorce called 'Any Matter,' which quickly become the basis for virtually all divorces. They had extrapolated this from the second half of the phrase 'an indecent matter' in Deut 24.1.

Jesus was asked if he agreed with 'Any Matter' divorces and said that the phrase in Deuteronomy only meant 'Indecency.' He added that if anyone got divorced for 'Any Matter' (unless it was a matter of 'Indecency') they were not really divorced, so they were committing adultery if they remarried.

Jesus also disagreed with many other Jewish presuppositions about marriage and divorce. He used the Old Testament to teach monogamy and lifelong marriage. He did not deny divorce, but pointed out that it should only be resorted to when a partner is hard-hearted, ie stubbornly breaking their marriage vows. He therefore denied that divorce was compulsory for unfaithfulness. He also denied the idea that marriage and procreation was a command so he would not support a divorce on the grounds of infertility. Jesus did not say anything about the other grounds for divorce—neglect of food, clothing and love.

Paul, however, did allude to these three grounds when he reminded the Corinthians that marriage includes the obligations of emotional support (1 Cor 7.3–5) and material support (1 Cor 7.32–35).

Paul told believers that they must not use the no-fault divorce-by-separation and told any believer who had already separated that they must attempt a reconciliation. However, he recognized that if they had been divorced by an unbeliever, there was nothing they could do about it, so he said that they were 'no longer enslaved.'

This was as close as Paul got to stating that remarriage is allowed, though his readers did not really need Paul's permission. Remarriage was such a firmly established right, in both Jewish and Graeco-Roman law, that it would require a very definite statement in the New Testament to convince them otherwise. In fact it was illegal for a Roman citizen to remain unmarried for more than 18 months after a divorce[27] (though this law was rarely enforced) so Paul would have had to tell Christians to break the law if he had forbidden remarriage.

The overall emphasis of both Jesus and Paul was that marriage should be life-long, and that divorce should be avoided whenever possible. A Christian should never be the cause of a divorce by breaking marriage vows, and should try to forgive a partner who has broken the vows, unless the partner is stubbornly unrepentant. Both Jesus and Paul condemned the no-fault divorce of their day.

Within a couple of generations, the church had lost all knowledge of the Jewish background of the gospel divorce debate and consequently thought that Jesus condemned all remarriage as adultery. The Jewish background of Jesus' divorce teaching was partially rediscovered in the mid-1800s. Since then, virtually all commentaries have mentioned the Hillel and Shammai debate but the churches have not yet applied this insight to practical theology.

5

Applying the First Century to the 21st Century Church

Marriage Vows in Christian Weddings

Traditional church teaching has only one ground for divorce—lack of sexual faithfulness—but the wording of the traditional Christian wedding service contains references to the other biblical grounds for divorce (neglect of 'love, food and clothing'), which were originally the basis of the marriage vows.

The oldest English liturgical tradition is preserved in the *Use of Sarum*, the most complete and influential of the early versions of the English liturgy which was drawn up in about 1085 by Osmund, Bishop of Salisbury. This is an amalgamation of the ancient Latin and early English ceremonies, which became the basis for the modern marriage service. In the Latin portion, the man vows to 'esteem, honour, keep, and protect' while the woman vows to 'obey, serve, esteem, honour, and protect.' This was derived from the wording of Eph 5.28f where husbands are told to love, feed and clothe their wives, just as Christ does:

> [28] Even so husbands should love their wives as their own bodies. He who loves his wife loves himself. [29] For no man ever hates his own flesh, but nourishes [literally 'feeds'] and cherishes it [literally 'keeps warm,' *ie* 'clothes'], as Christ does the church.
>
> (Ephesians 5.28f)

---

27   The *lex Julia* and *lex Papia* mentioned on page 7 above.

Ephesians has changed the more legalistic language of Exod 21.10f ('love, feed and clothe') into more caring terms ('love, nourish and cherish'). Ancient Jewish marriage contracts also avoided legalistic language, and used terms like 'esteem, honour, protect.' This same type of language found its way into Christian marriage vows, which can therefore be traced back to the grounds for divorce in Exod 21.10f.

The English portion of the *Use of Sarum* adds to these basic vows by having the wife promise:

> I N take thee N to my wedded housbonder to have and to holde from this day forwarde for better: for wors: for richer: for poorer: in sykenesse and in hele: to be bonere and buxum in bedde and at the borde tyll dethe us departhe, if holy chyrche it wol ordeyne, and thereto I plight the my trouthe.

Most of these additions have survived, except the wonderfully alliterative 'be bonny and buxom in bed and at board,' which originally meant 'be obedient'—'bonny' meant 'good,' 'buxom' meant 'pliant,' and 'in bed and at board' meant 'night and day.' The reference to obedience is probably due to the context of Eph 5.28f. Obedience was never a marriage vow in the Old Testament, though it did become a marriage vow in first-century Judaism and Christianity, because this was a necessary part of secular morality and it would have been a scandal to omit it. Whether or not this was also part of specifically Christian morality is too large an issue to discuss here.

Most Christian marriage services are based on this ancient Latin and early vernacular English liturgy. This means that virtually all married Christians have vowed before God and the congregation to love, feed, clothe and be faithful to their spouse. Although we do not use these exact words, because liturgical language has become somewhat more elaborate, our vows are nevertheless based on Eph 5.28f, which is in turn based on Exod 21.10f. This means that our marriage vows include all the Old Testament vows which were affirmed by Jesus and Paul, and which were the basis for divorce in the first century.

Pastoral Implications

The Graeco-Roman 'divorce-by-separation' was similar to the present day separation of couples who live together without a marriage ceremony. The Jewish 'Any Matter' divorce was similar to the modern 'no-fault' divorce of married couples. In neither case was there any need to cite grounds for a divorce, just as there is no need to cite grounds in most modern divorces. Despite these similarities, it is not easy to apply the first century documents to a 21st century church.

Before we can apply the New Testament, we have to read it in its cultural context in order to try and understand what it meant to its original recipients. This raises questions about the authority of Scripture and tradition. In this study we have found that a first-century reader would have a different interpretation to that of a modern reader. This conclusion can be unsettling in itself, because people may wonder what else the church has got wrong. Therefore the church been very cautious in attempting a re-interpretation of Scripture on this topic, even though much of what is presented here has been well known in the scholarly community for more than a century.

During the history of the church there have been many more serious doctrinal disputes, such as the Trinity, the Mass, Apostolic succession and, more recently, female leadership, gifts of the Holy Spirit, and the nature of scriptural inspiration. These are more theologically fundamental than the doctrine of divorce and re-marriage, though it might be said that they have fewer direct consequences for public morality.

Several practical questions arise from this study, a few of which will now be examined briefly.

Should the church teach against no-fault divorce, which is now the main type of divorce in the UK, USA and other countries, and teach specific grounds for divorce?

Before 1937 it was very difficult to get a divorce in Britain, though one could, theoretically, get a divorce for adultery. New grounds or 'offences' such as cruelty, desertion, insanity or long terms of imprisonment were introduced in The Matrimonial Causes Act 1937, which also made divorce a much cheaper and easier process. The Anglican Church report *Putting Asunder*[28] recommended that the principle of 'irretrievable breakdown' of marriage should supplant the concept of 'matrimonial offences.' This was implemented in the Divorce Reform Act 1969 which defined 'irretrievable breakdown' by a series of 'proofs' such as mutual separation for two years. The Family Law Act of 1996 attempted to remove the need for proof but was found to be unworkable.

The direction of legislation has therefore been away from specific grounds for divorce and towards a 'no-fault' divorce system. The same trend has occurred in the USA since the first 'no-fault' bill was introduced in California in 1969. The number of divorces has risen dramatically, though there is still a debate about whether this is due to the lifting of restrictions, or whether public morality has changed.

Christians are confused. The church teaches against divorce, but it provides no solution for those who are suffering physical and emotional abuse within their marriage. Many Christians have concluded that the Bible is impractical and unfair in this area, so they have used the law of the State as a basis of their morality instead. This confusion would be ended if the church taught a practical set of grounds for divorce.

---

28 SPCK, London, 1966.

Should the church teach the Old Testament grounds for divorce—unfaithfulness, material neglect or abuse and emotional neglect or abuse, which were affirmed by Jesus and Paul (according to this study)?

The 'traditional' grounds (adultery and desertion by an unbeliever) have the advantages of being the 'plain' reading of the text, as well as the consistent teaching of the church for many centuries. However, they are impractical, and leave a large minority of believers suffering abuse within marriages or feeling guilty when they are divorced.

In my opinion, the church should teach *all* the biblical grounds for divorce. These can be taught on the basis of marriage vows so that they are seen within the traditions of the church. The church should teach that marriage vows form grounds for divorce if they are stubbornly and unrepentantly broken.

Should those who remarried after an invalid divorce get divorced again and re-marry their original spouse?

Jesus' and Paul's teaching appear to give different answers. Jesus said that a person who remarried after an invalid divorce was technically committing adultery. Paul, on the other hand, told the person who had been divorced-by-separation (an invalid form of divorce) that they were free from that marriage.

Paul does not give any reason except: 'God has called us in peace.' He is probably referring to the technical rabbinic phrase 'for the sake of peace,' which means 'when the law fails, we follow a pragmatic solution, for the sake of peace.'[29] Paul could have argued that the deserted person was suffering neglect of 'food, clothing and love,' so they had valid grounds for divorce. But instead, he took the pragmatic view that the divorce had happened and was irreversible, so the marriage was over.

In the light of Paul's view, we need to look again at Jesus' conclusion. It is possible that Jesus was merely stating the logical outcome of remarriage after an invalid divorce, in order to show how serious it was. This is similar to his conclusion that a person who mentally commits adultery is guilty of actual adultery. Presumably mental adultery was not a literal ground for divorce. Similarly technical adultery, due to an invalid divorce, would not be a literal ground for divorce.

Therefore, although divorce without valid grounds is wrong, it still marks the end of a marriage. The person who divorced without valid grounds should repent before God, and if neither partners have remarried they should seek reconciliation. However, if either partner has remarried, they should not compound the wrong by breaking up yet another marriage.

---

29   David Instone-Brewer, 'Techniques and Assumptions in Jewish Exegesis before 70 CE,' *Texte und Studien zum antiken Judentum*, 30 (Tübingen, J C B Mohr, 1992).

Should the church allow remarriage of 'innocent' divorcees after divorce on a biblical ground?

The inability of 'innocent' divorcees to remarry has been a constant problem for the church. Even in the severe climate of the Early Church Fathers, there were several instances of Christian remarriages after divorce for unfaithfulness.[30]

It is only the indissolubility argument which makes it impossible for an innocent divorcee to remarry. As shown above, the command 'let no man separate' implied that divorce was possible, not impossible, and the Pauline passages which speak about the end of marriage through death do not rule out divorce. Virtually all the Reformers allowed remarriage for the innocent partner, and even Augustine said that such remarriage was 'not a grave sin.'[31]

The concept of indissoluble marriage has very shaky scriptural support, and makes even innocent divorcees into guilty sinners. Therefore the church should stop teaching this uncertain doctrine and should instead emphasize the sinfulness of causing divorce by breaking marriage vows.

Should the church allow remarriage of 'guilty' divorcees and those who used 'no-fault' divorces?

Remarrying a 'guilty' divorcee might imply that their sin does not matter. However, if only the 'innocent' can remarry, this implies that breaking marriage vows is an unforgivable sin. And if the church decides to remarry only the 'innocent,' it will have to set up some kind of court to establish innocence and guilt. In my experience this is often impossible, because one person is rarely completely innocent.

In pastoral practice I have remarried divorcees only on the condition that they take part in a service of 'Repentance for Broken Promises.' I have conducted this as a prayer service for myself and both prospective partners, even if one of them is not divorced. We confess together that we have broken promises which we have made before others and God. I have never tried to ascertain whether a divorcee is innocent or guilty and no-one has ever asked to be excused from this service. A form of words which might be used is:

All: Heavenly Father, you have cared for me from my birth, and you have promised to love me unconditionally; I come to you in repentance. I confess that I have made promises to you and to others which I have not kept. I have promised to love and care for others, and I have not

---

30 Ambrosiaster specifically allowed this (*Commentary* on 1 Cor 7.15), and perhaps Tertullian (*Marcion* IV.34). Epiphanius (*Heresies* 69) and the Council of Elvira (canons 8 and 9) regarded it as a lesser evil than unchastity. Some Fathers openly doubted the sinfulness of such remarriage (Augustine, *On Faith and Works*, Acw No 48; Origen, *Matthew*, II.14.24), while others criticized churches who had allowed such remarriage (Justin *Apol* 2.2.1–8; Origen, *Matthew*, II.14.23; Jerome, *Letters*, LV *To Amandus* 3–4).

31 'It is not clear from Scripture whether a man who has left his wife because of adultery, which he is certainly permitted to do, is himself an adulterer, if he marries again. And if he should, I do not think that he would commit a grave sin'—Augustine, *On Faith and Works* (Acw No 48), as cited in Deasley, Alex R G, *Marriage and Divorce in the Bible* p 205.

fulfilled this as I should. Please forgive me for my sin, and give comfort to those whom I have let down and hurt. I ask you for strength for the future, to be able to keep the promises which I will make. Amen.

Minister: (A prayer for the couple's wedding and future life.)

This has been extremely well received, especially by those who probably were 'innocent.' Ideally this service occurs after the wedding rehearsal, in the same place where they will take their marriage vows the following day. This makes the prayer particularly poignant and, according to some couples, makes them feel as though the past is behind and that God will help them not to make similar mistakes.

Conclusions

Recent advances in our understanding of the New Testament world means that we can now read the divorce and remarriage texts more clearly through the eyes of a first-century believer. This 'first century' interpretation suggests that Jesus and Paul taught against no-fault divorce, and allowed divorce on the biblical grounds of unfaithfulness, material neglect and emotional neglect. Jesus affirmed the first ground and Paul affirmed the others. They also allowed remarriage after a valid divorce. Both emphasized that a Christian should never be the cause of a divorce by breaking their marriage vows, and Jesus suggested that a believer should always forgive and be reconciled to a repentant partner who breaks their vows.

The church lost touch with the Jewish background at a very early stage due to the supremacy of the Hillelites after the destruction of Jerusalem, and the separation of the church and synagogue. The traditional interpretation (divorce only for unfaithfulness or desertion by an unbeliever, without the right to remarry), has caused great suffering for a large minority. The state now allows divorce on a no-fault basis (through separation), and some Christians are using this because they regard the church teaching as impractical.

The biblical grounds for divorce have been preserved in the Christian marriage ceremony. The biblical principle is that divorce is permitted when marriage vows are broken, but the sinner is encouraged to repent and their partner is encouraged to forgive them. Remarriage is possible after a divorce, but the sinfulness of breaking former marriage vows should be expressed in some way.[32]

---

32 For further reading, see my *Divorce and Remarriage in the Bible* (Eerdmans, 2001) and other resources at www.Instone-Brewer.com. For a completely different viewpoint, see W Heth and G Wenham, *Jesus and Divorce* (London: Hodder & Stoughton, 1984, Carlisle: Paternoster, 1997).